For Nikki, for being the Catlyst to my Quest. For my Mother, for always pushing me to be ME; and for my tribe (you know who you are) this is for anyone seeking a reminder of our inherent relativity to on another.

BE YOU

Profound Whatever.

Introductions

Proufound Whatever is my attempt to share what I have felt, and tried to express,
during moments of my life that have helped unfold some kind of epiphany, or radical relative network.
Psychdelic, in its etymology, means to make/manifest mind. Every artist does just that.
With the words, art pieces, and schemes formed;
It is nothing short of the schemes in mind-manifestation.
    The act of trying to express the seemingly inexpressible (while creating a subjective relativity that thrives) is what a huge part of what art is about.
Communication is an art form.
It is my humble hope that these visuals,
and linguistics provoke a profound feeling/notion that you carry onto the next person you interact with;
To share the experience of our human commonality.
    The way the art was thrown together, is the onlt scheme to PROFOUND WHATEVER.
The Art and poems are not exactly related to each other in this book.
As my first publication,
my mistakes will be a muse for progress and will allow attention to the lesson of growth.
 We stumble while learning to walk, it's how we keep it moving.

   Thank you so much for existing, for witnessing the documentations of my past/present tenses in the now.
How strangely beautiful it all is.

THANK YOU

Communicate;LISTEN,EXPRESS, and TALK TO ALIENS,

-STAY WILD-

Profound Whatever.

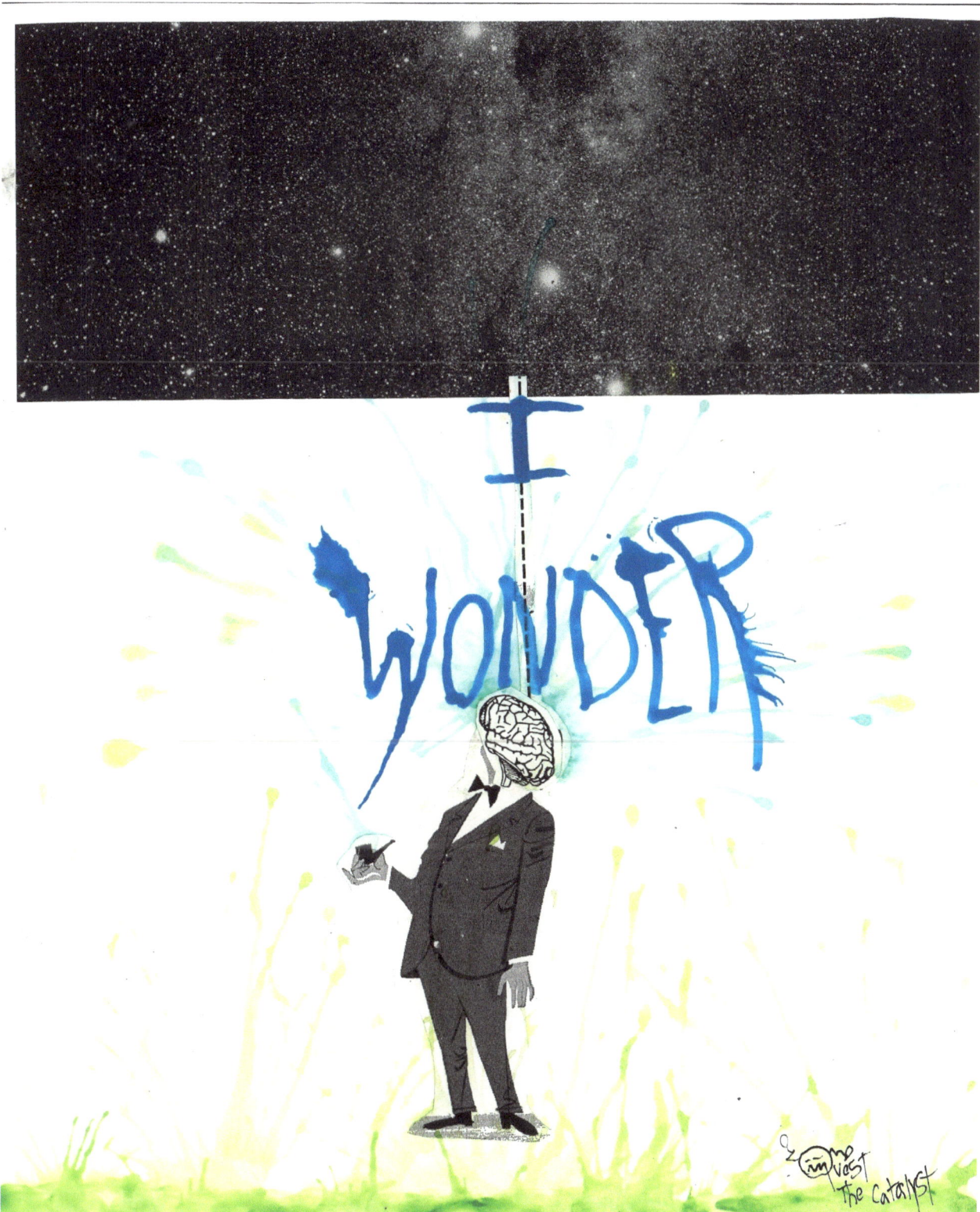

"I wonder" Collage/Watercolor/Paintmarker

Profound Whatever.

SQUARE ONE

The dirt and the seed,

Square One,

and this bloody tee.

Cleaned up with dust, from stars half way on my way to where you are,

back at the start,

around and around,

back home and on the road.

Constantly carrying my bag of bone.

Yet when i've roamed, I found new things known.

Seen stuff grow.

And I myself found new raods,

new woes, new joys, and new reasons to

GO.

Profound Whatever.

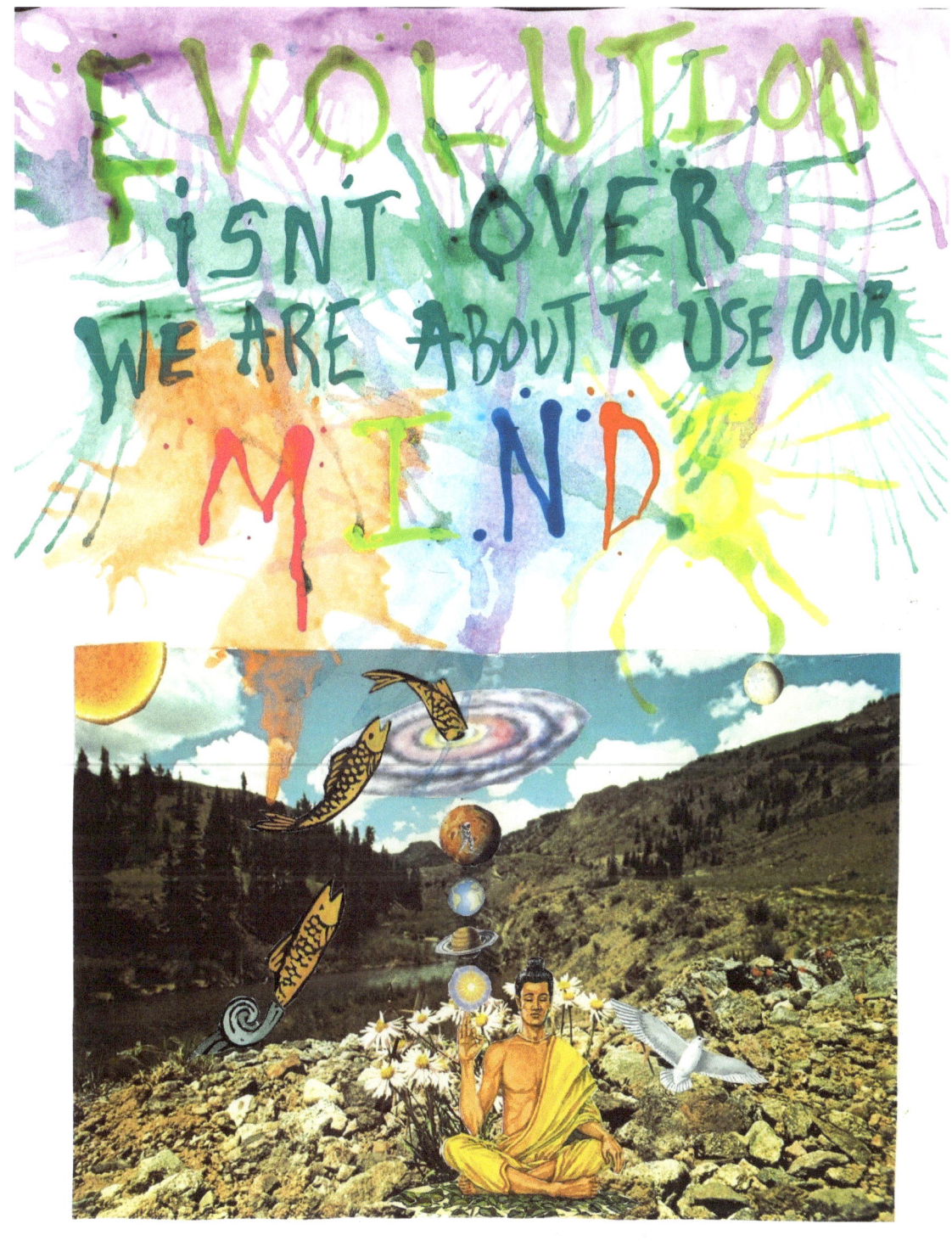

"Evolving still" Collage/Watercolor/Paintmarker

Profound Whatever.

This Thing

We feel it,
the way we are.
We ponder it and what it means.
The skin I occupy,
the brain is use.
The I,
and what it sees.
How much of me am I, and am I you too?
I love to witness you, for it brings me a comparative.
A **spectrum**.
Im thankful you exist.
It keeps me alive.
I know you see me too, and we dance.
Maybe we will never dance again.
Everything we ever were and are;
Defined by the moments we manifest
through the items behind our chest.

They Call it: **FRIENDS**.

They call this **FRIENDSHIP**

Profound Whatever.

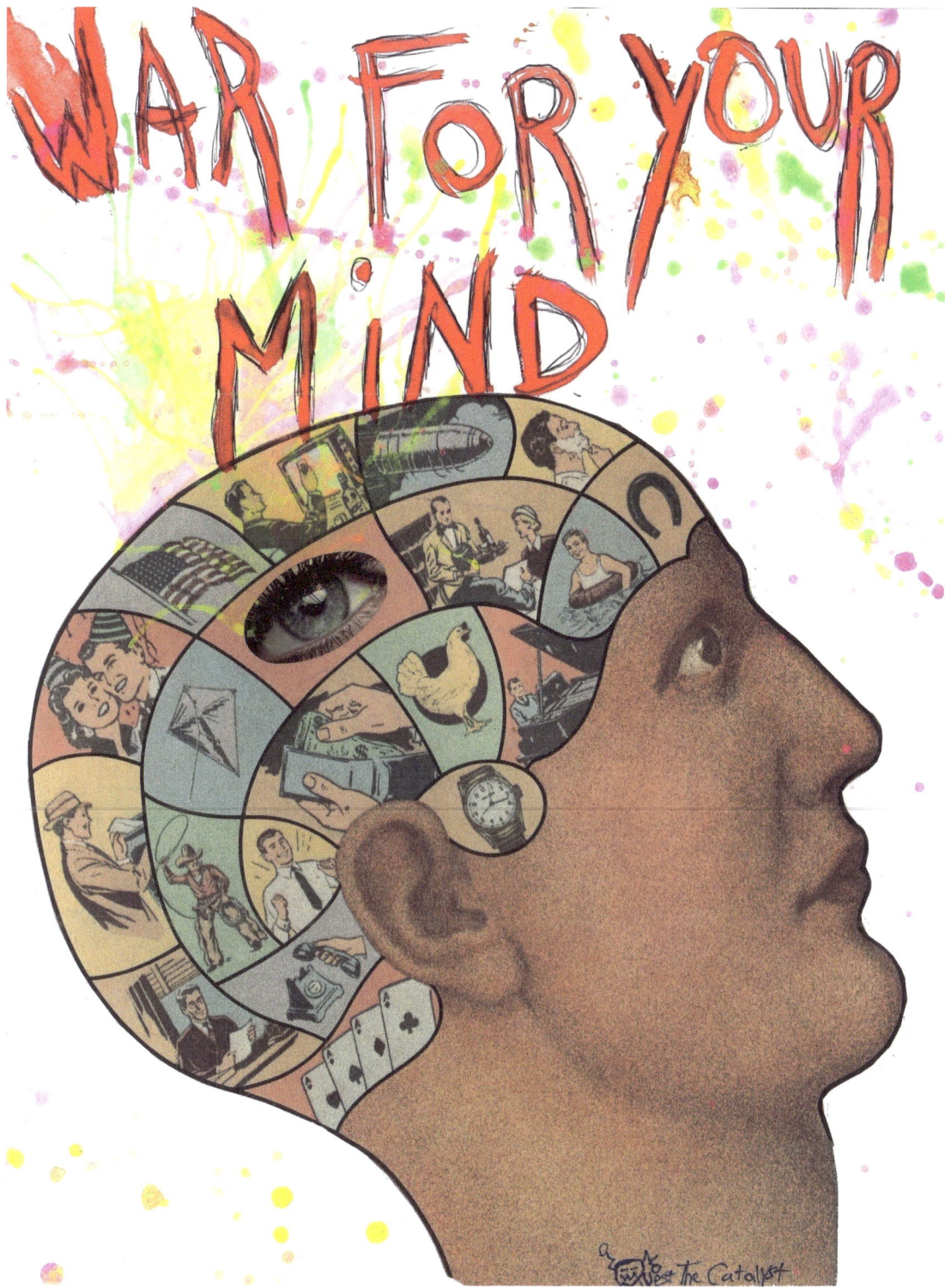

"here is a war on for your mind" Collage/Watercolor/Paintmarker

Profound Whatever.

Wandering about it

Ive outgrown your doom.
I've grown in too soon,
Inward I bloomed,
It blossomed too soon.
"Not soon enough" said the bearer of bad news.
I wouldn't bet a dollar on your attitude,
It's as transient as the wind.
Then again,
You wondered why I'd wave.
It's a fun ride, even with goodbyes.
The way you straddle memories with the shoes of your soul.
I found a paintbrush.
How many subjects.

Switch

Switch

Switcheroo.

If ya don't stop, you'll make somethin' new.

New wave on hazy days and the ways our arms wave, "this way!"

It's not just yours.
This is the thing that we made

Soup,
I like soup.
It's warm, and wholesome,
And inclusive.

We are still primordial.

We are futuristically prehistoric,
We're dismal and euphoric.

We're almost there,

So please, fucking FLOOR IT .

Profound Whatever.

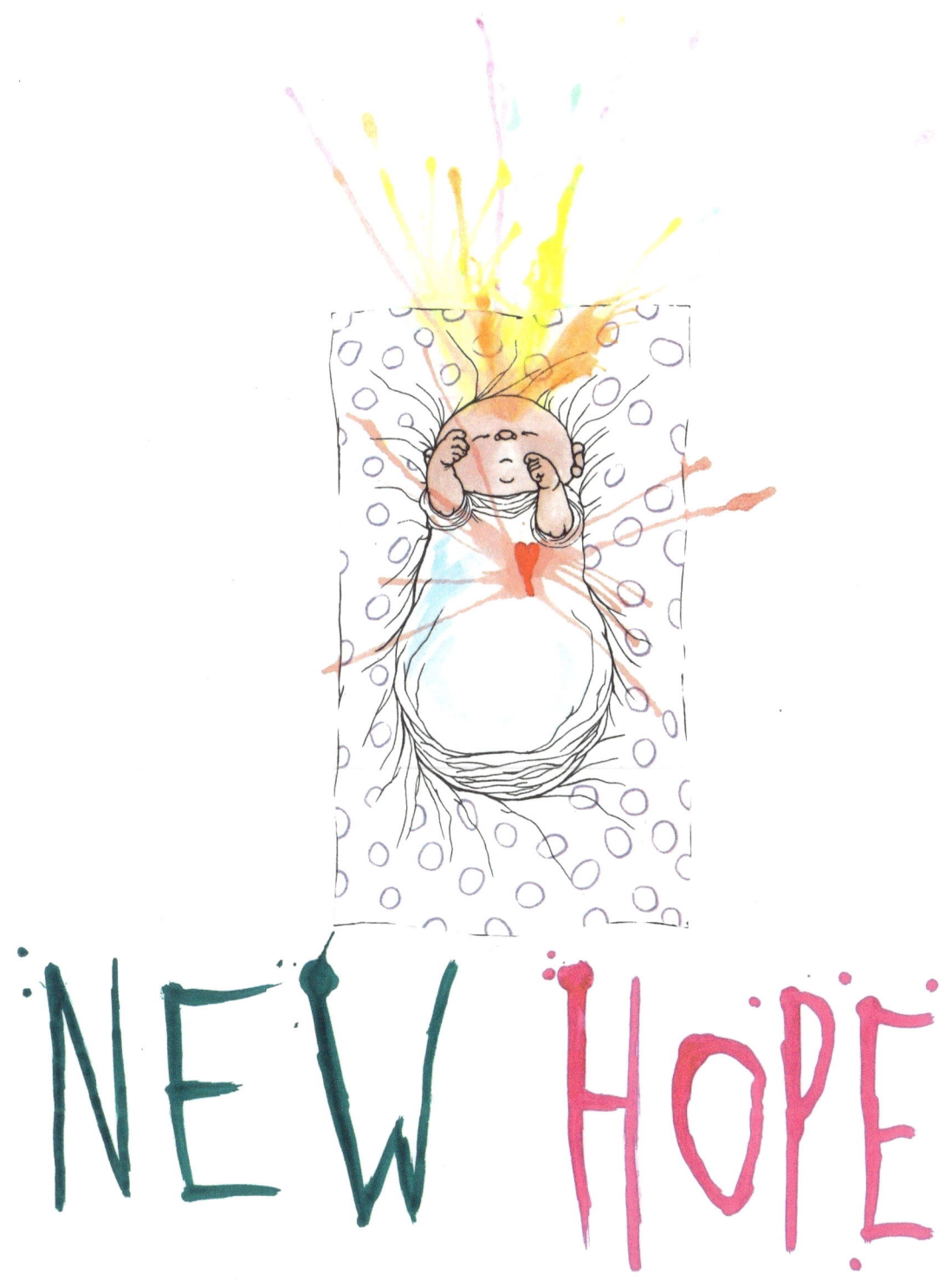

"New Hope" Collage/Watercolor/Paintmarker

An extension of Yours

There is much to touch, to hold, to love.

Let the ball point pens express

    it, as does the keyboard for the modern age.

        An electronic perspective,

            still connected by the primordial hands,

        hands that touch these tools from pen to motherboard.

Open your minds forever, because things are constantly changing.

    Shannon Hoon said it to me and you to use.

        Just like it was said by the family **crow**,

            as one,

            together,

            let us grow.

            Can I help?

            Can you help me?

            Can we see?

            let us, all three.

Profound Whatever.

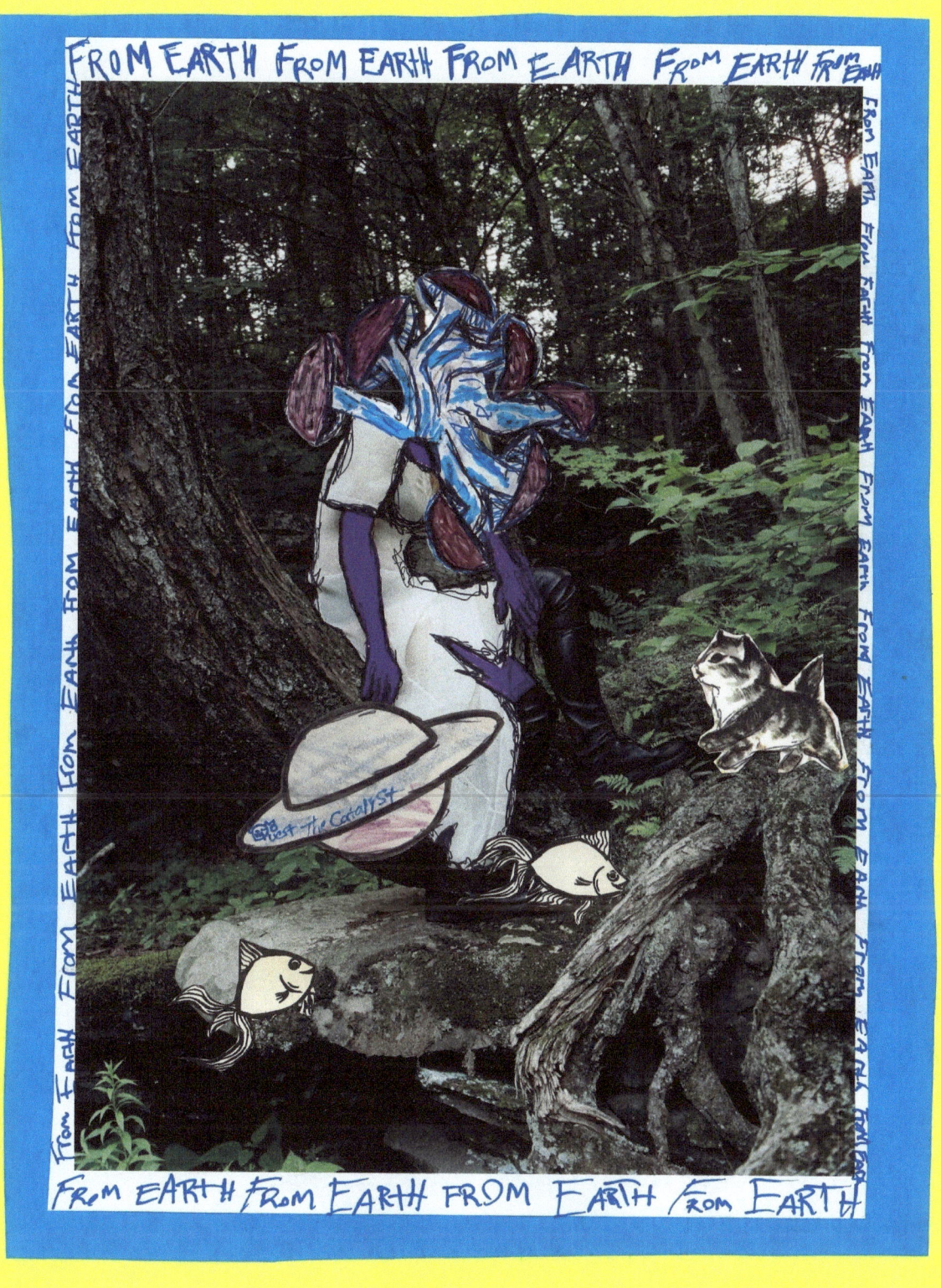

"From Earth" Collage/Ink

Profound Whatever.

Questionless Answer

Memory jaunts.
"You got what it takes," they say.
The sound was something well deserved.
A picture to cure the craving.
Lovers dance, and haters fight.
It's the sleeping of mind in the comfort of the night.
"Oh well," they say, "well wake up again."

Kiss the thought that you'd be cool under the light.
you're sweating profusely.
Nervous, twitching, twiddeling.
I'll count it down.
I'll write out.
I spit it out.
My tongue will shape the words I thought about.
There's something in what she says, that eases all the thoughts.
Something in the answer that had no question.
I'm dancing out of excitement.
Shouting out of pleasure.
Letting all the balloons with helium into the endless sky.
Watch...
watch..
until they disapear.
Does it always go away?
When do they pop.
How long before all of it just falls back down to where it started.
Gravity has its way of teaching you a lesson.

Profound Whatever.

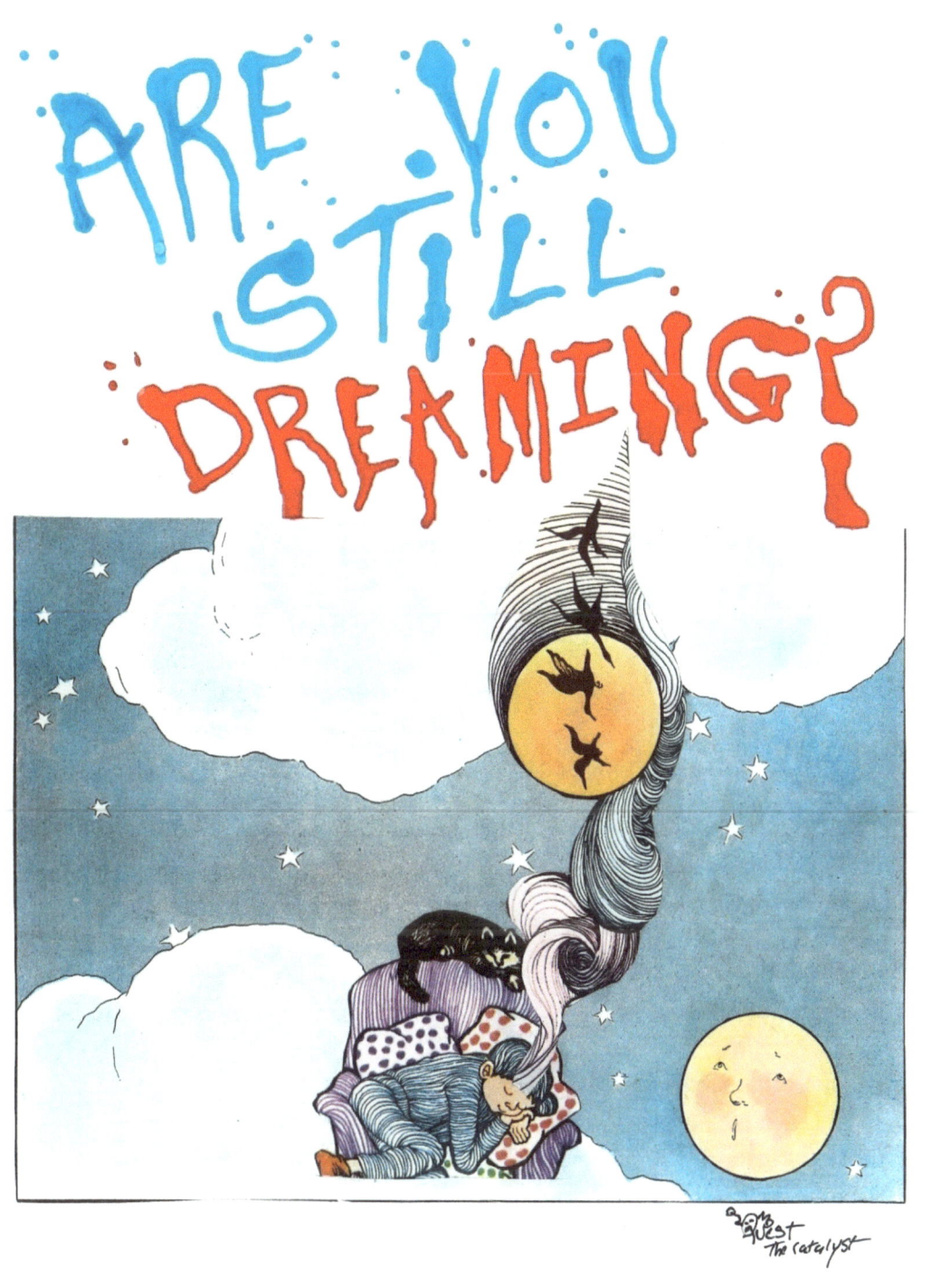

"Dont quit your daydream" Collage/Paintmarker

Profound Whatever.

Lesson of the season

Summers end,

Upon my face.

The things we said, did, and meant.

The fall and how it loves tomorrow.

The soil, and what it gives, that we then borrow.

And the joy, of right now,

Prevents us from the sorrow.

Profound Whatever.

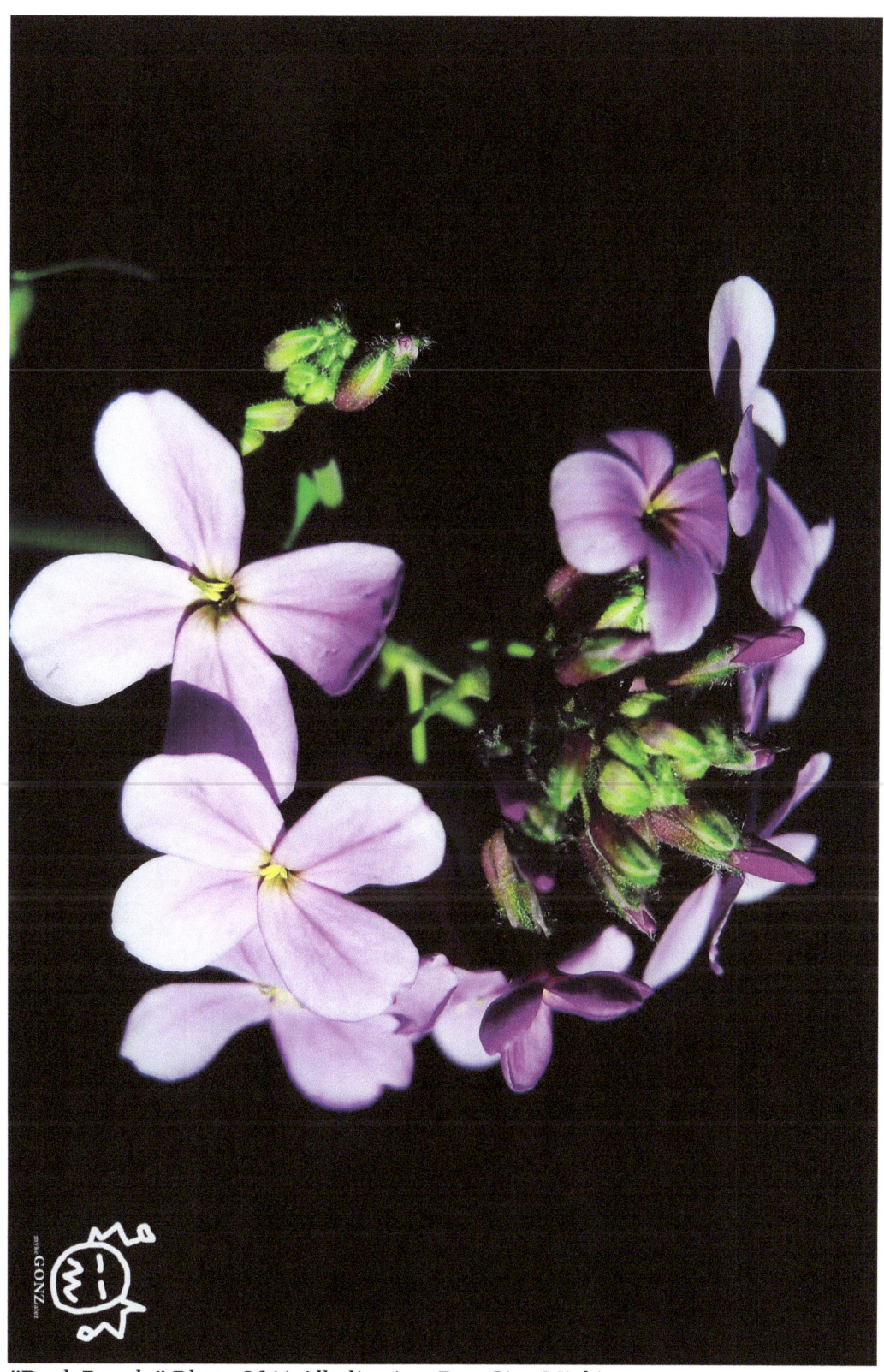

"Dark Purple" Photo 2011 Alkali ruins, Bay City, Michigan

Snap out of it

Let's pretend she's a man.
      So you can be more present,
be more authentic.

      Let's pretend you dont want to **hold** her hand for at least just one minute.
      Let's pretend her lips don't rest perfectly against each other like two crescents.

    Perhaps we could forget for the moment, the beauty that resonates from the scents of her body.

And lets be honest, the shape of her breasts.

    Let's escape the distractions of your presence that entagles my **present** in a slew of 'what ifs' and 'just maybes.'

      Let's revert,
    put my hands aside.

Forget your *magic* as it trades spaces with the atmosphere around this room.

Let's forget you are here, and remember you when it's fair.

Profound Whatever.

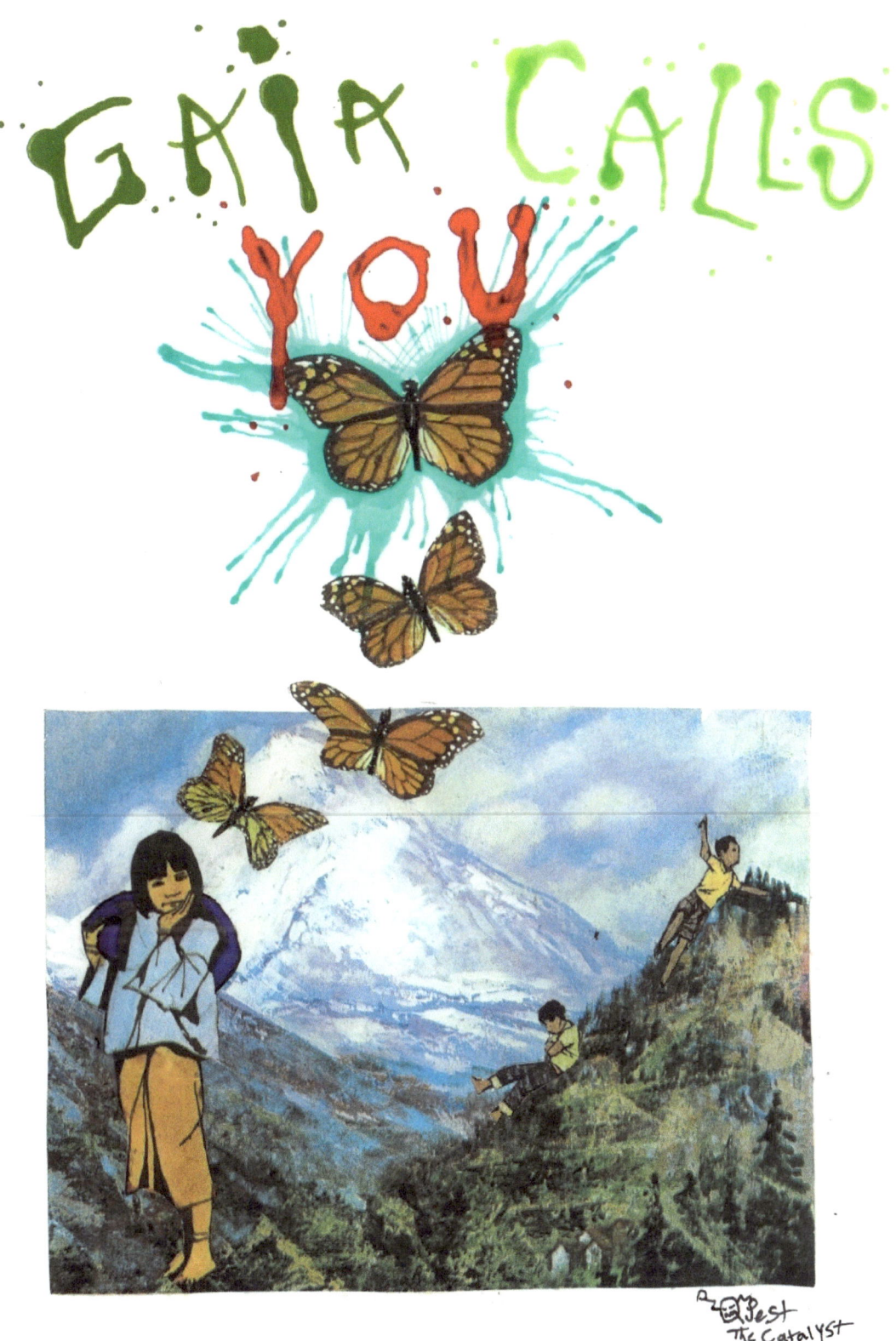

"Go to her" Collage/Watercolor/Paintmarker

Getting to know You

Dont be surprised at how beautiful you are:

Riding in cars,

sitting in bars,

pettin' kitties,

sniffin' flowers.

The manuscript of your minutes,

                 and the artist of your hours.

Don't be surprised at how long it takes,

to realize all your powers,

and the weapons at hand.

To cultivate the dreams that you see.

The visions that capture you,

and the one that never stops calling you…

even now, the one you hear begging you to do whatever.

Whatever it may be within you that makes you,

YOU.

Profound Whatever.

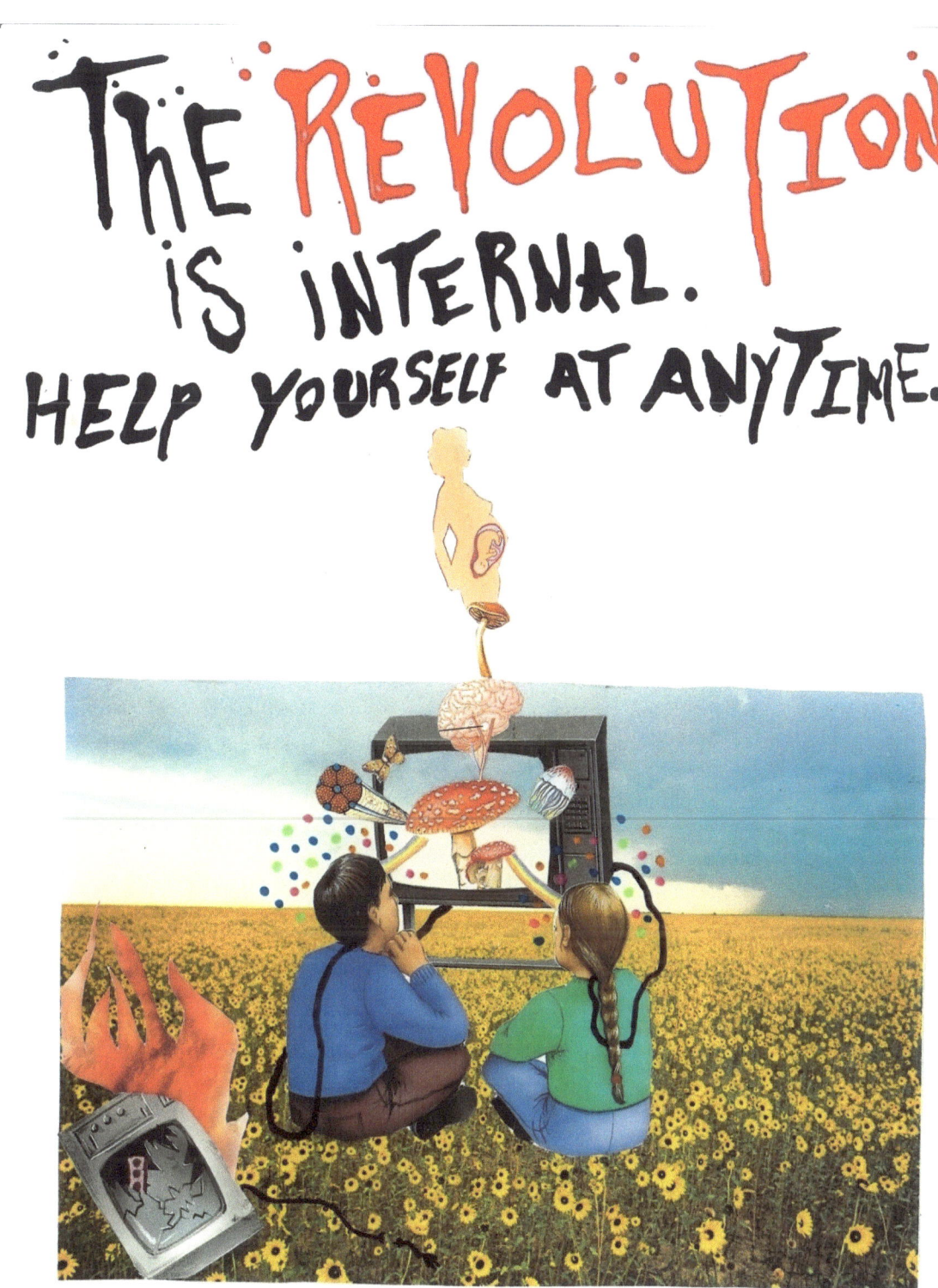

"Help Yourself" Collage/Watercolor/Paintmarker

Further

Nomadic if you must.

A thwarting of the comforts, of your trust.

Make it so you may not know, what?

Wonder what's next!

Take the armor from off your chest.

Put the pedal down.

Utilize the gasoline.

Take it at its best.

Don't wait.

Don't rest.

Ride the waves,

<u>take the quest</u>

Profound Whatever.

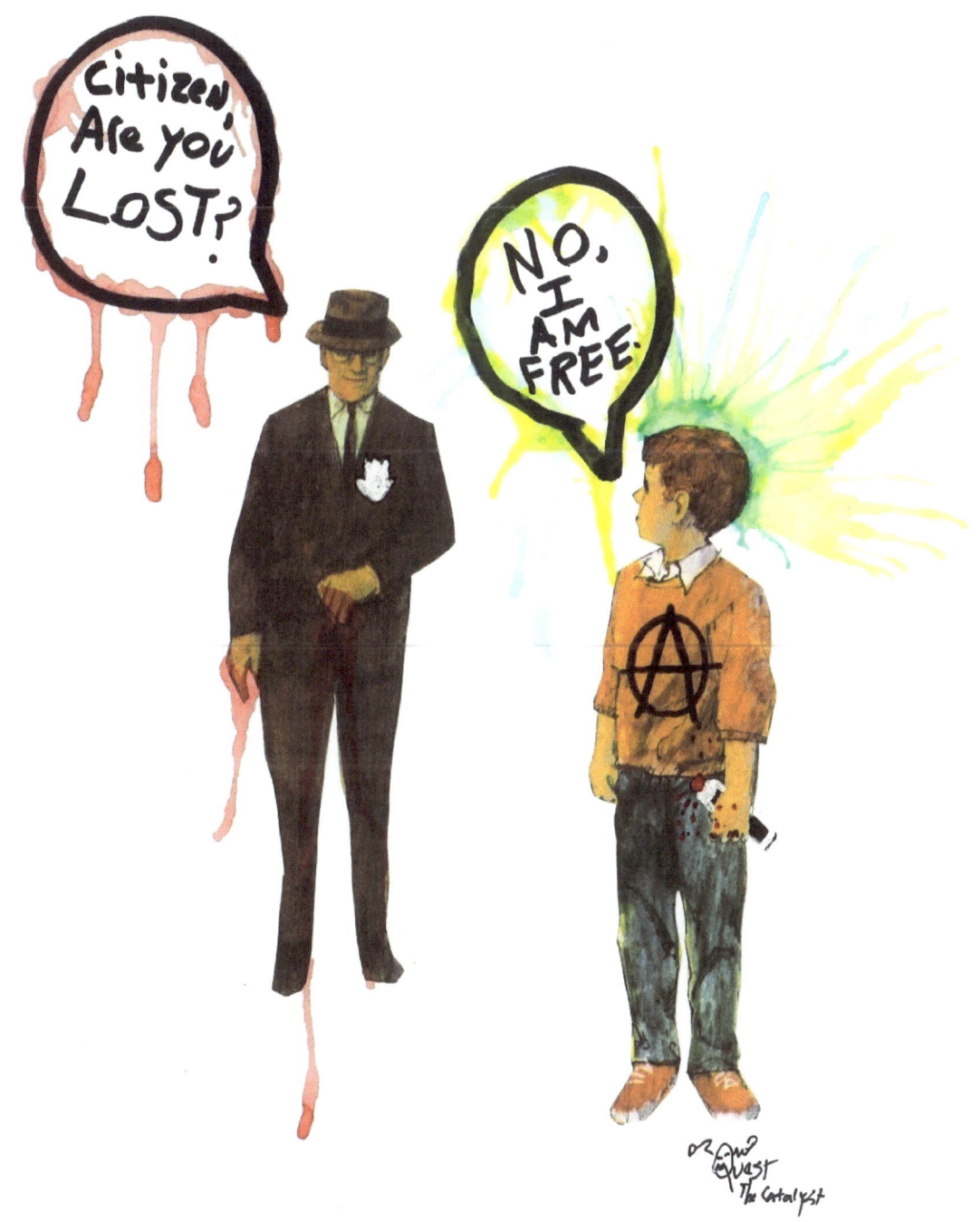

"Can i live?" Collage/Watercolor/Sharpie

Procrastinator

This is lazy.

The way we stare at our projects,

watiing for the inspiration to take hold.

How bold it is to be patient,

while knowing each second that passes,

we are getting older.

How cold it can be to turn our shoulders,

and avert the mess.

the dreams don't wait.

We shouldn't rest so much that lethargy clogs us up.

Profound Whatever.

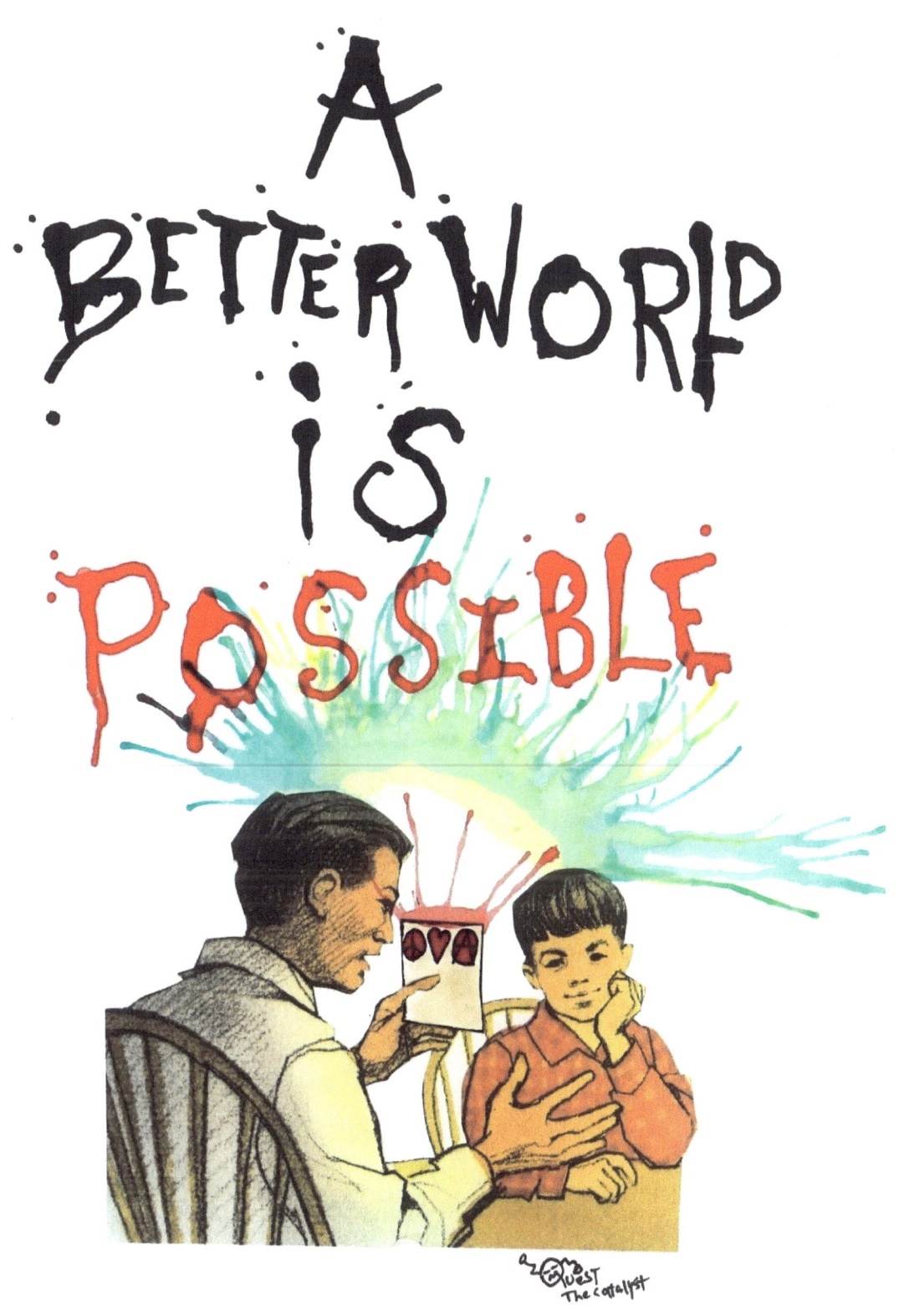

"Tell yo Kids" Collage/Watercolor/Paintmarker

Work it

I am working

this is working.

We are working this out,

the way that we doubted the things that we found.

We are shedding our frowns

for a pleasant experience of 'the now.'

How beautiful, it's true,

the way we manifest the meaning from our hearts,

and heads, through expressions,

in an attempt to connect.

To flow our love.

The flow state of what we love.

The lessons of our relativity.

No, not just me.

No, not just you,

but everyone is a witness.

Every fucking one of you;

So, be provoked to document the present tense.

Be inspired to play that role,

by the passions built into your body.

You are working,

look at you go,

doing all of this,

and you might not have even known.

So take deep breaths, let it be shown,

that you are in control enough to let go.

That your are in control enough to just let it flow.

Profound Whatever.

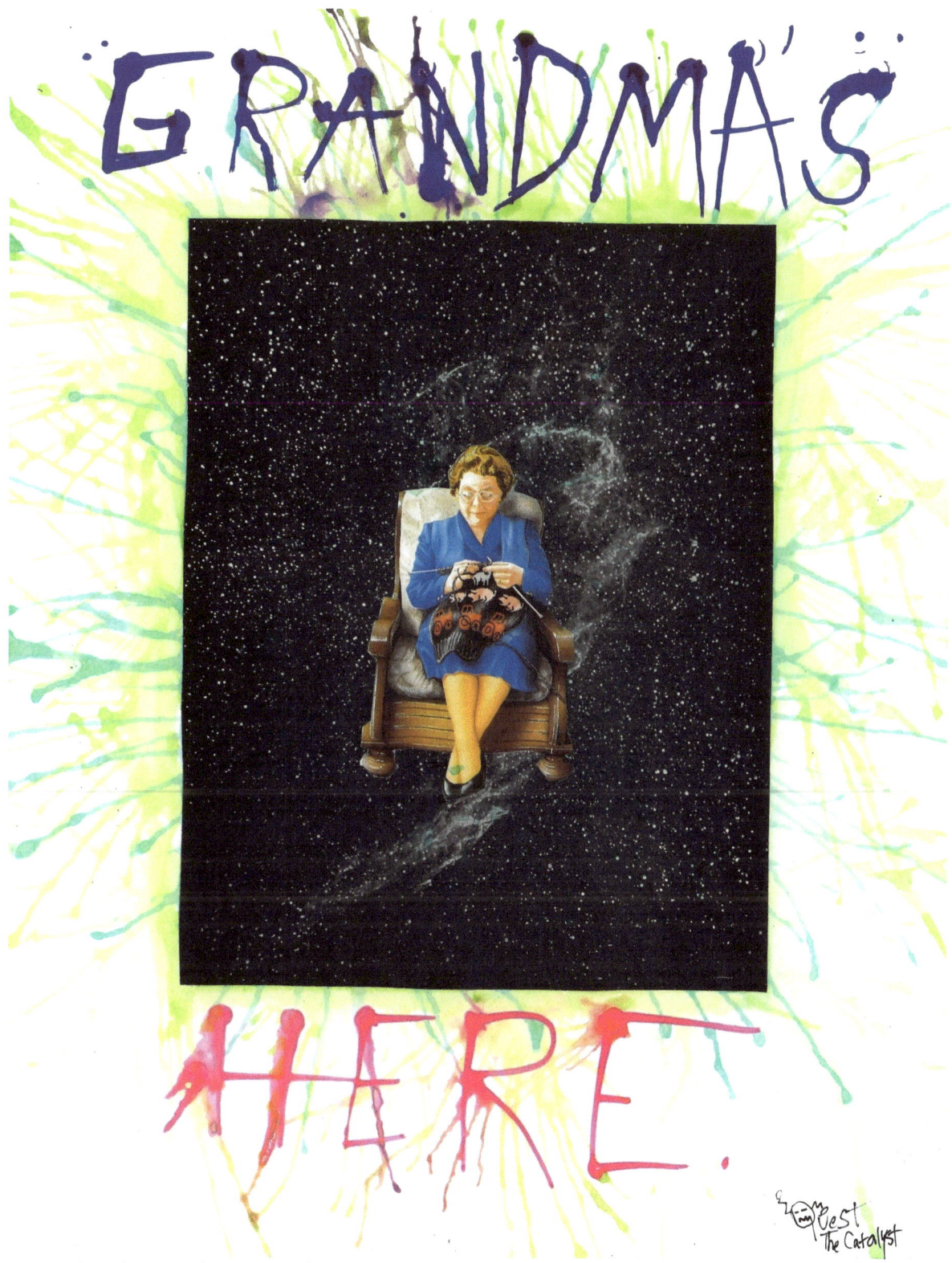

"Grandmother Medicine" Collage/Watercolor/Paintmarker

THIS THING

I am quite certain,

that this is real.

The way we can cultivate the things we dream of.

The way we manifest the things we speak.

And I am quite confident that we all can do this.

Make moves.

Create change.

Make sense

I am fully invested in the truth of our ability,

to shine the sun,

to hear the sound,

to use our own lungs.

We do this thing.

We are this thing!

Profound Whatever.

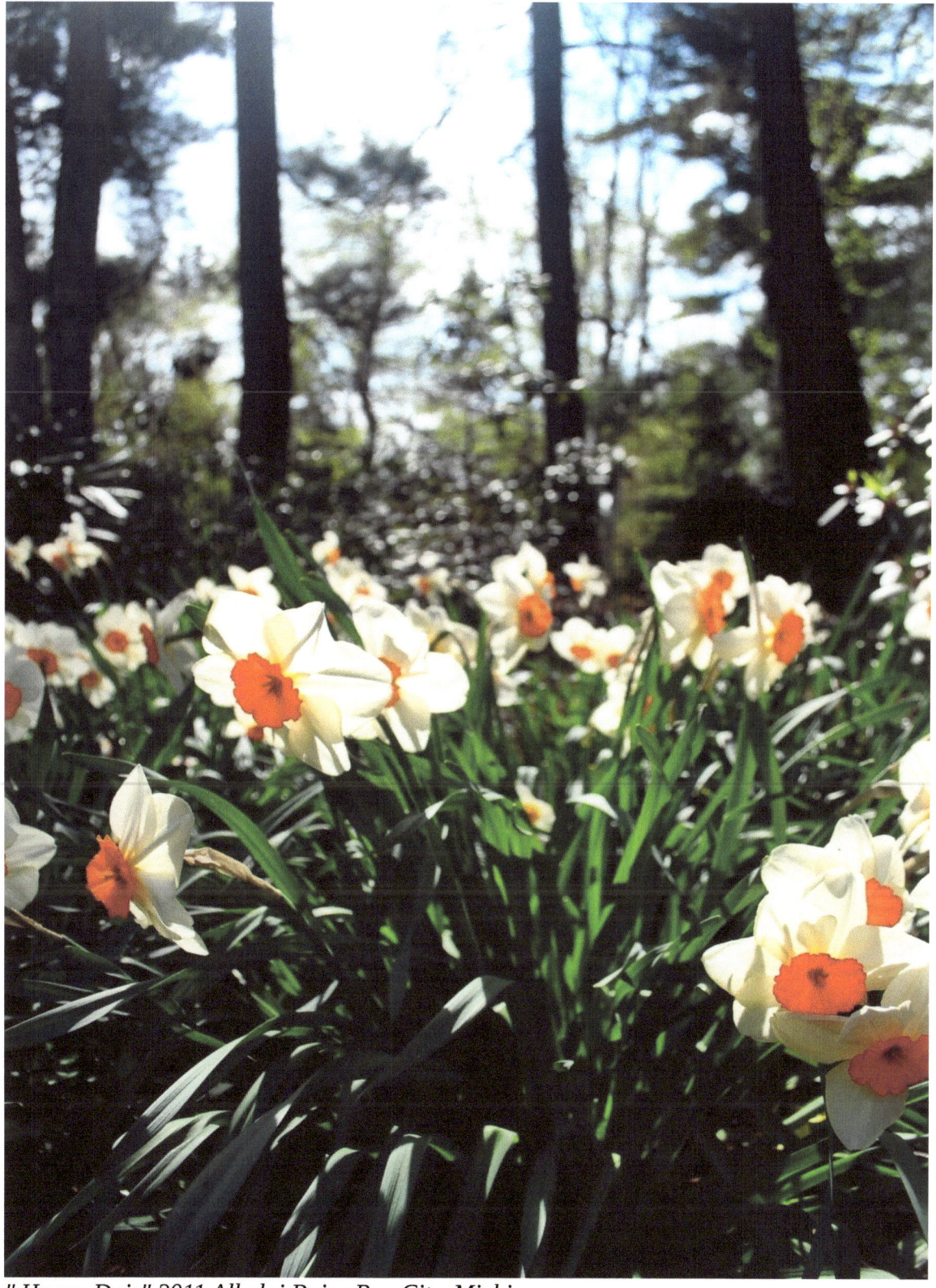

" Happy Dais" 2011 Alkalai Ruins Bay City, Michigan

Profound Whatever.

Adriana

We would pick flowers and ride bikes.

We would paint things, and cook some foods.

We would sing songs, and even play them too.

When you were a baby you needed me most, to just love you.

I loved loving you, I want to love you more, again.

Rub the space between your eyes until you sleep.

On day you will be so big.

I'll be proud.

And I know i'll miss you,

I miss everything already,

as soon as you leave.

but maybe,

we will still pick flowers, and paint stuff,

and cook things too;

And you will always be my child,

my biggest inspiration to be good,

to be human.

To be love, just like you

Profound Whatever.

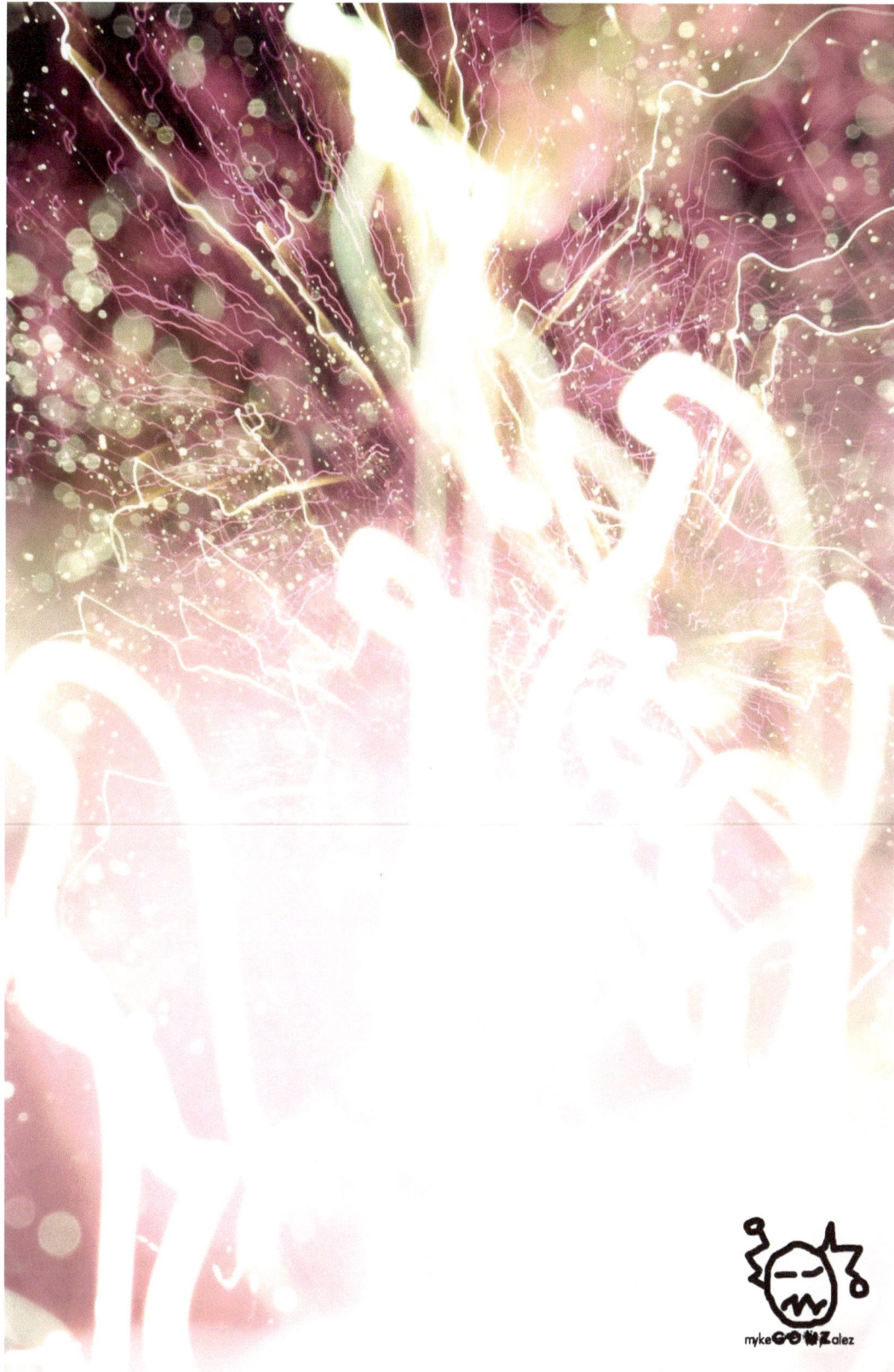

"Electric Mess" Photo of Bay City Fire Works in Long Exposure

I see,

no, I really understand.

Time to go home.

We gonna pack it up.

It's time to go.

No, I mean, it's really time to go.

Gonna think about you on the ride home.

Gonna get home, and feel,

confused that it's real.

Another one has been taken,

by Babylon.

Goodbye,

Babylon.

Profound Whatever.

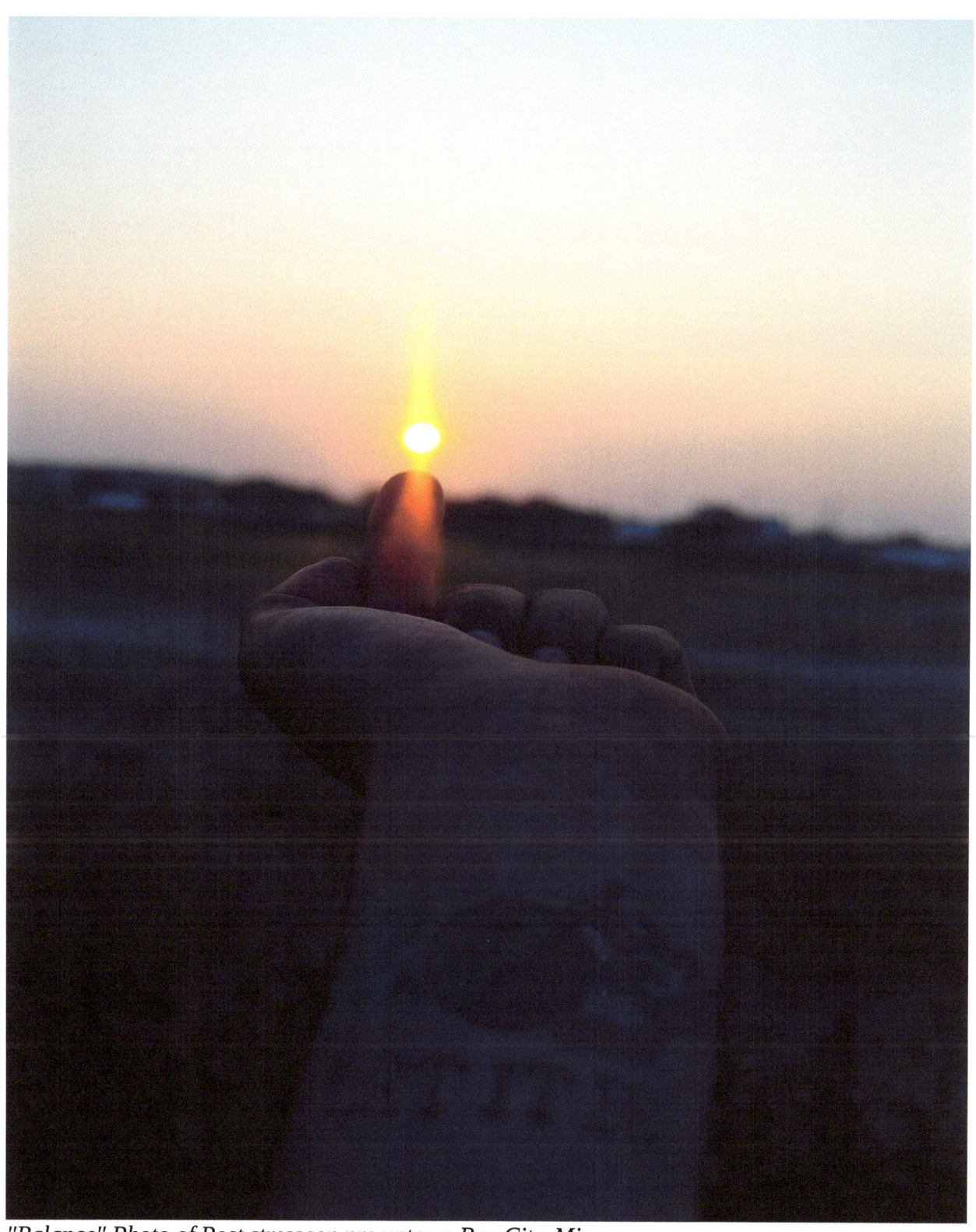

"Balance" Photo of Post stresscon pre uptown Bay City, Mi

Fragment

I am a fragment little human,

waiting on you to pull me back together.

I think I know you better anyway, it's true.

Seems like the unit is in unity,

with the unification of this universe,

and everything is my university.

I know.

And every time I think I listen,

I'm listenin'…

I'm trying to figure out where you are coming from,

what your narrative is,

and why you're pointing your finger like a gun.

Profound Whatever.

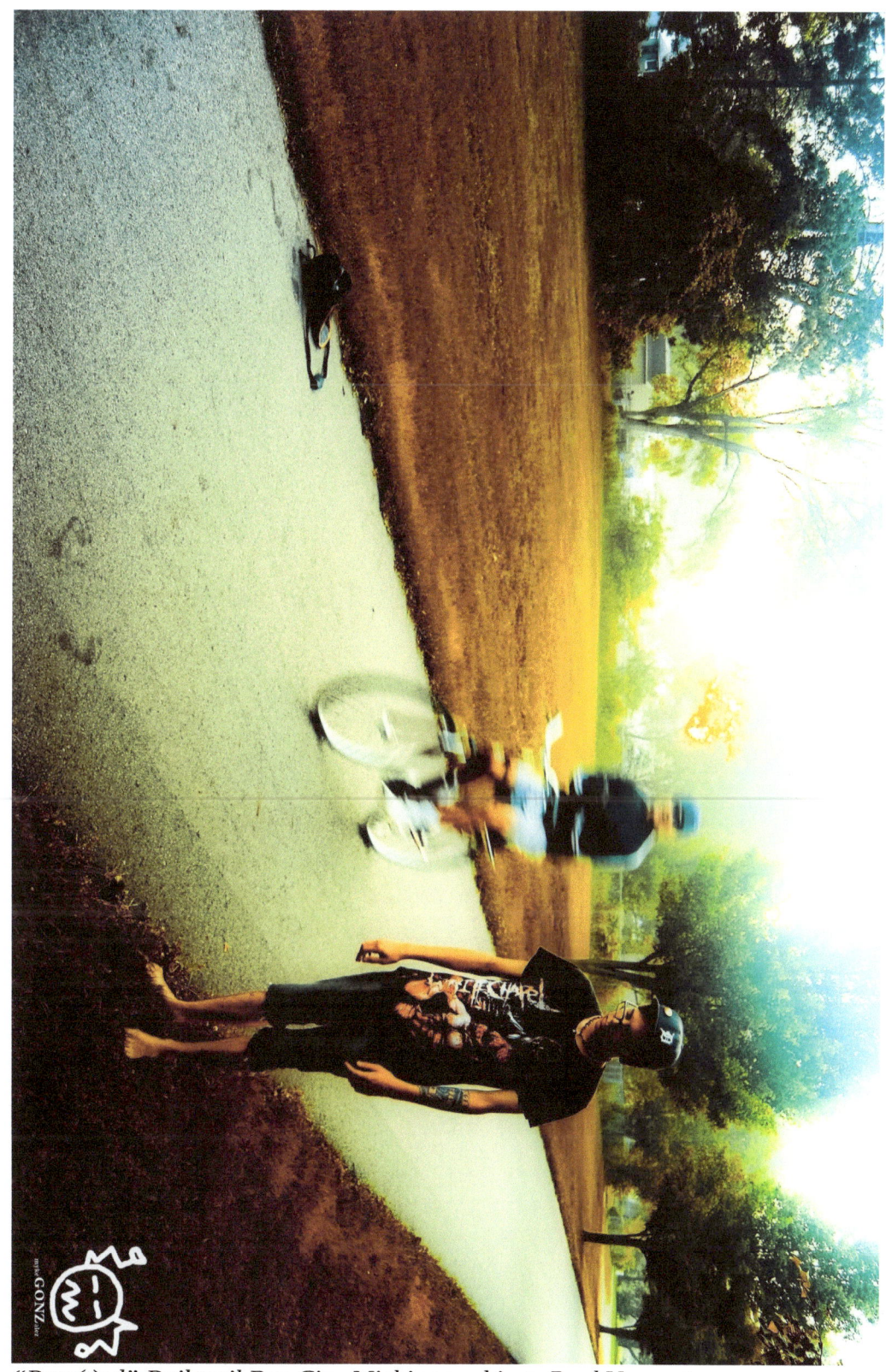

"Pass(t)ed" Rail trail Bay City, Michigan subject: Paul Vanwert

Grateful for the shapes of your face
and the angles that your body makes.
Arms over and under, the way we get together it's called a hug.
And there is always space. Right here between us.
I rolled my ankles trying to hurry up, thinkin'
'maybe if I get there fast,
it would be the best time I ever had.'
I lured away a mystery
for the answers to inquistions that beckoned me ,
to cultivate someone better.

You're gone now,
and so am I.
And so is this!

Profound Whatever.

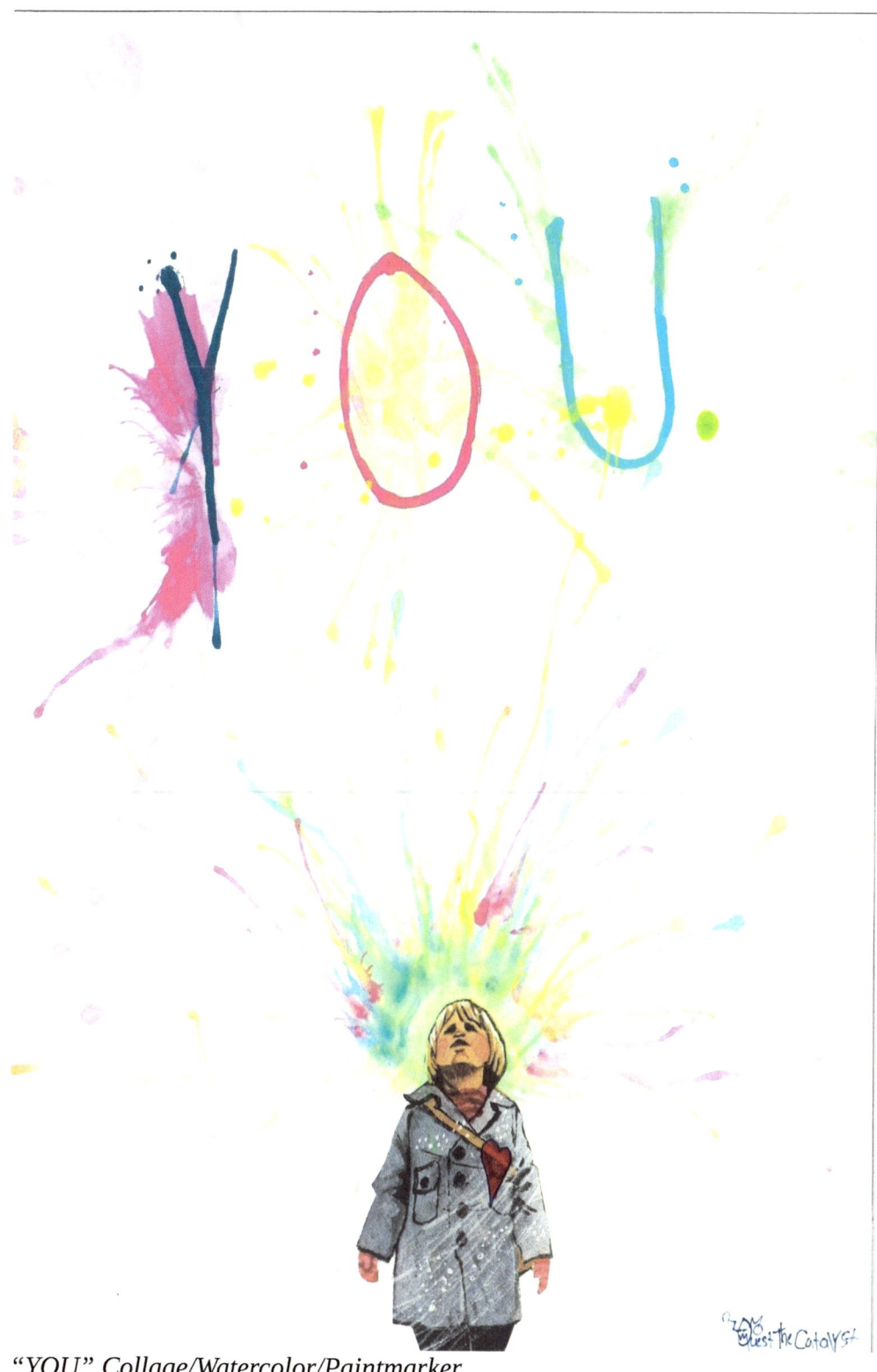

"YOU" Collage/Watercolor/Paintmarker

Profound Whatever.

To the man with rosy cheeks, and fists used, for fighting for the right things.

May the world be aware of all that you were, by the graces of your gifts, and all that was left.

The size of your smile, unmatched by anything ever measured by man.

The humor of your eyes, so giving to the others,

by virtue of laughter.

The loving nature of your soul, and how your arms carries us home.

That time you threw your fists up to stand up for a friend, the home you gave us when we were to stubborn to turn in.

The bum song, and the joy of you rvoice when you sang it. You left too soon.

Before any of us could repay you for every single ounce

of love you permeated with you brilliant heart.

Goodbye brother, you left a pressure on my chest.
  Goodbye brother, someday ill see you,
    and tell you about all the rest.

Profound Whatever.

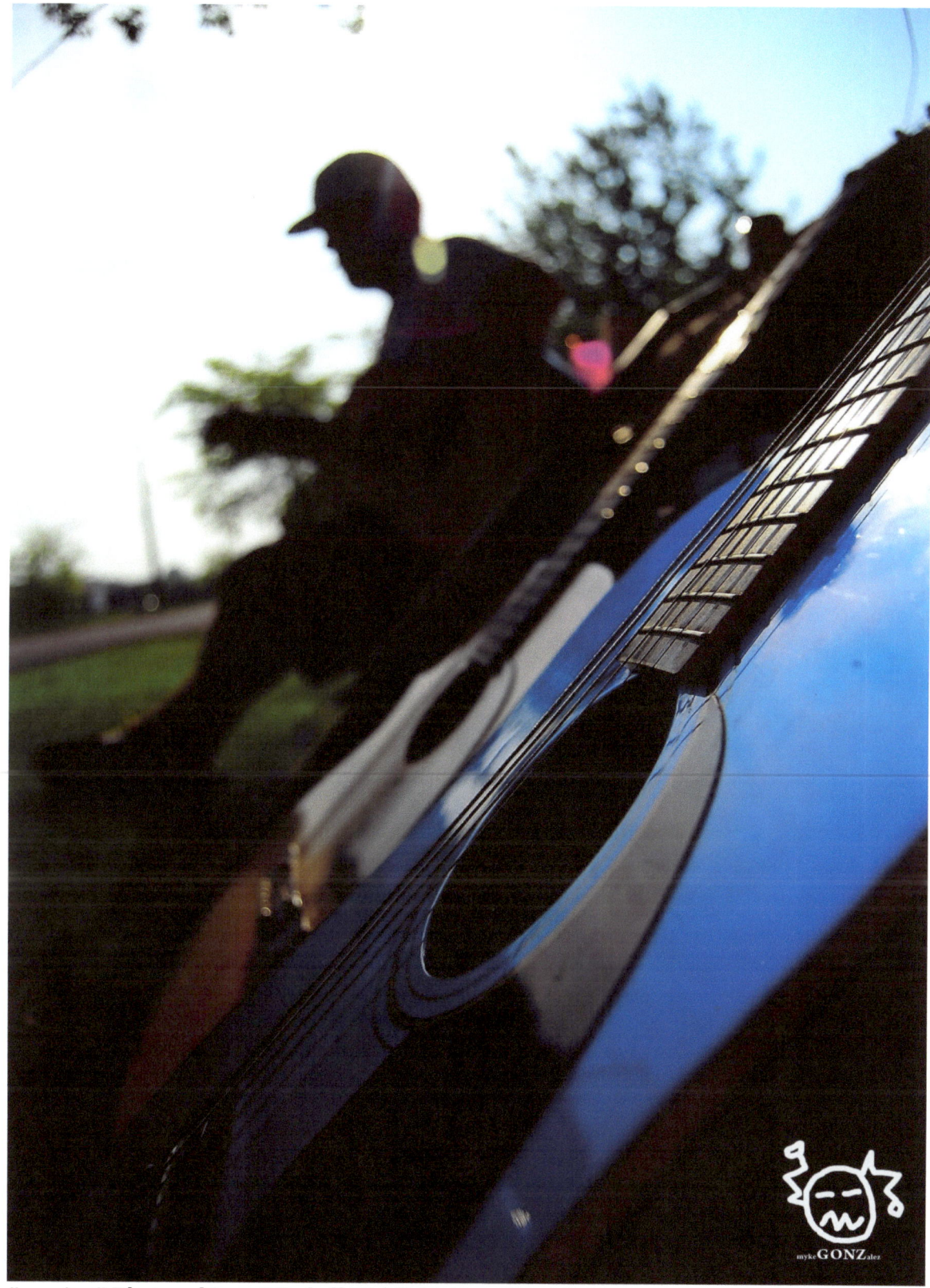

"passion" Photo subject: Mitchell Wahlfeldt Bay City, Michigan

Humbled.

Hungry.

Helpful.

Haunted.

Hurt.

Happy.

Have.

Have not.

Hurried.

Had to.

Have to.

Humbled.

Happy.

Helping.

Help me.

And Happy.

Happy Happy.

Happy Happy Happy

it has me.

Profound Whatever.

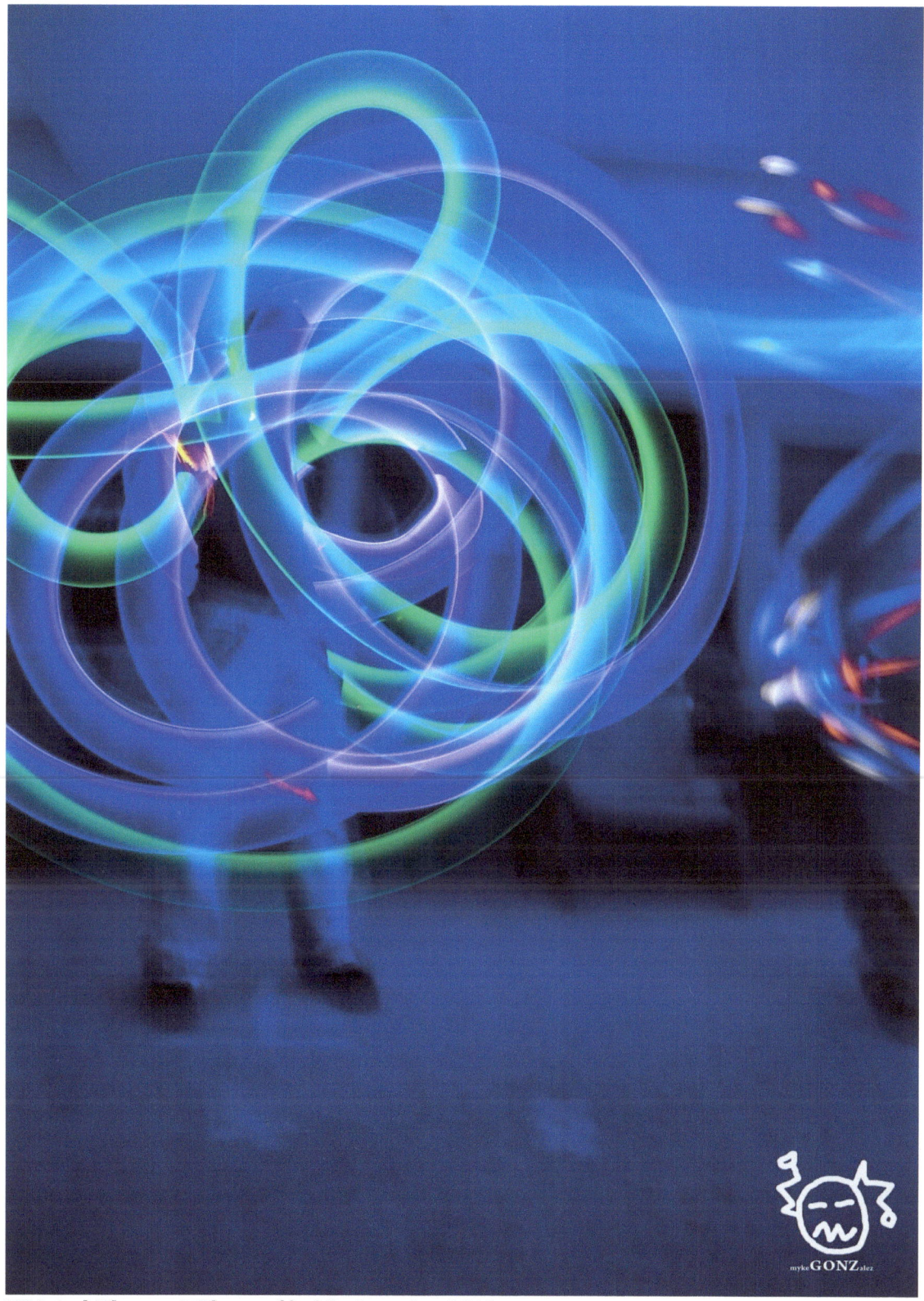

"Digital Flowers" Photo of led Poi at zday 2013

Wanderer and his eyes

Full spectrum,

let me see your flesh.

Who are you?

And are these things just tests?

Locomotive.

Keep it movin'.

The comfort of your breast.

The reason for compassion,

and its conjuring waves.

So inherently we have crests.

So inherently we wake up.

And inherently we rest.

Profound Whatever.

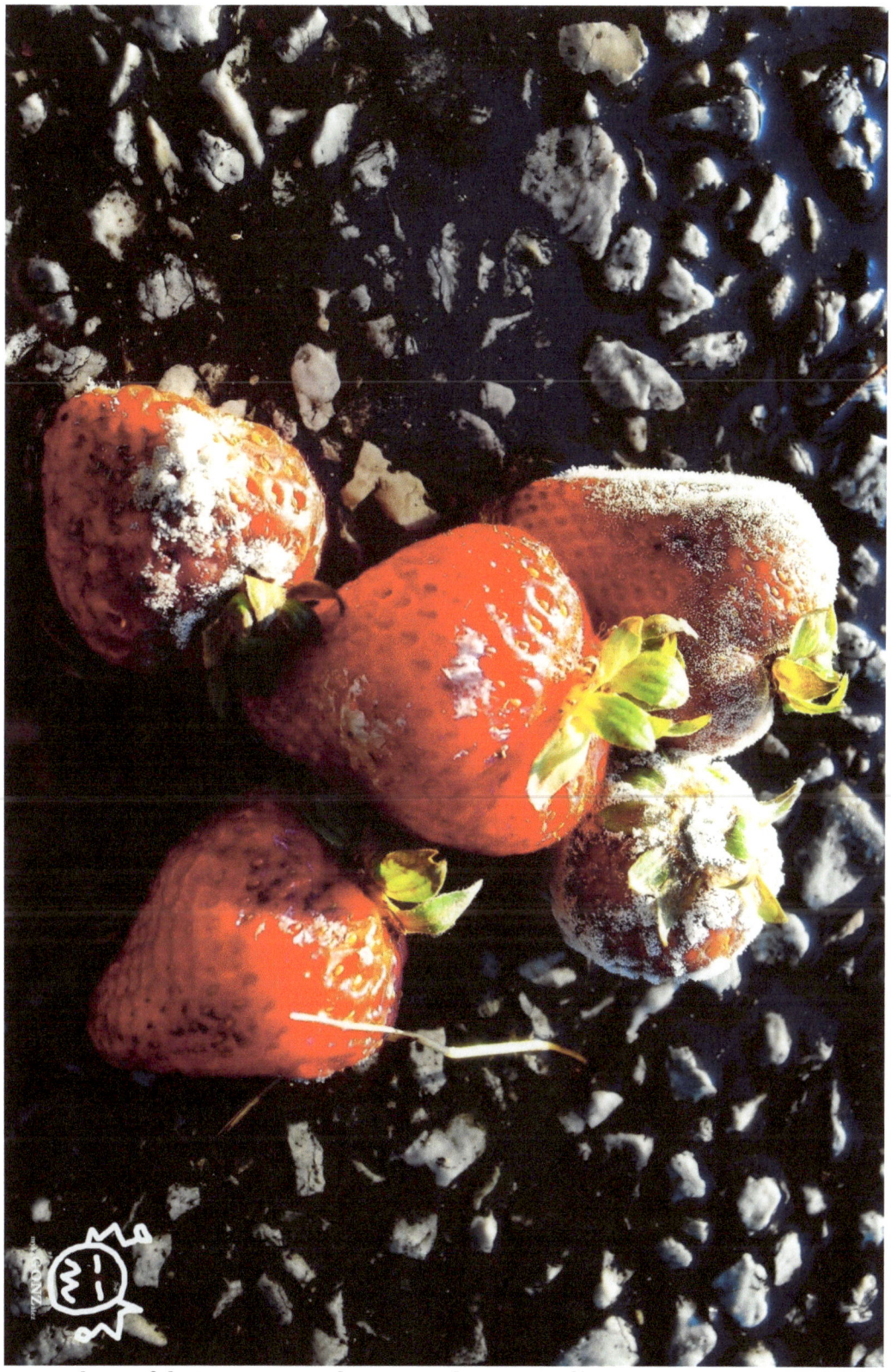

"Dirty beautiful" Rotting strawberrys on the strees of bay city, mi

Profound Whatever.

Shes here.

In a **yellow dress**, with **green** trim.

She touches my skin.

Her name is summer,

She's finally here.

Profound Whatever.

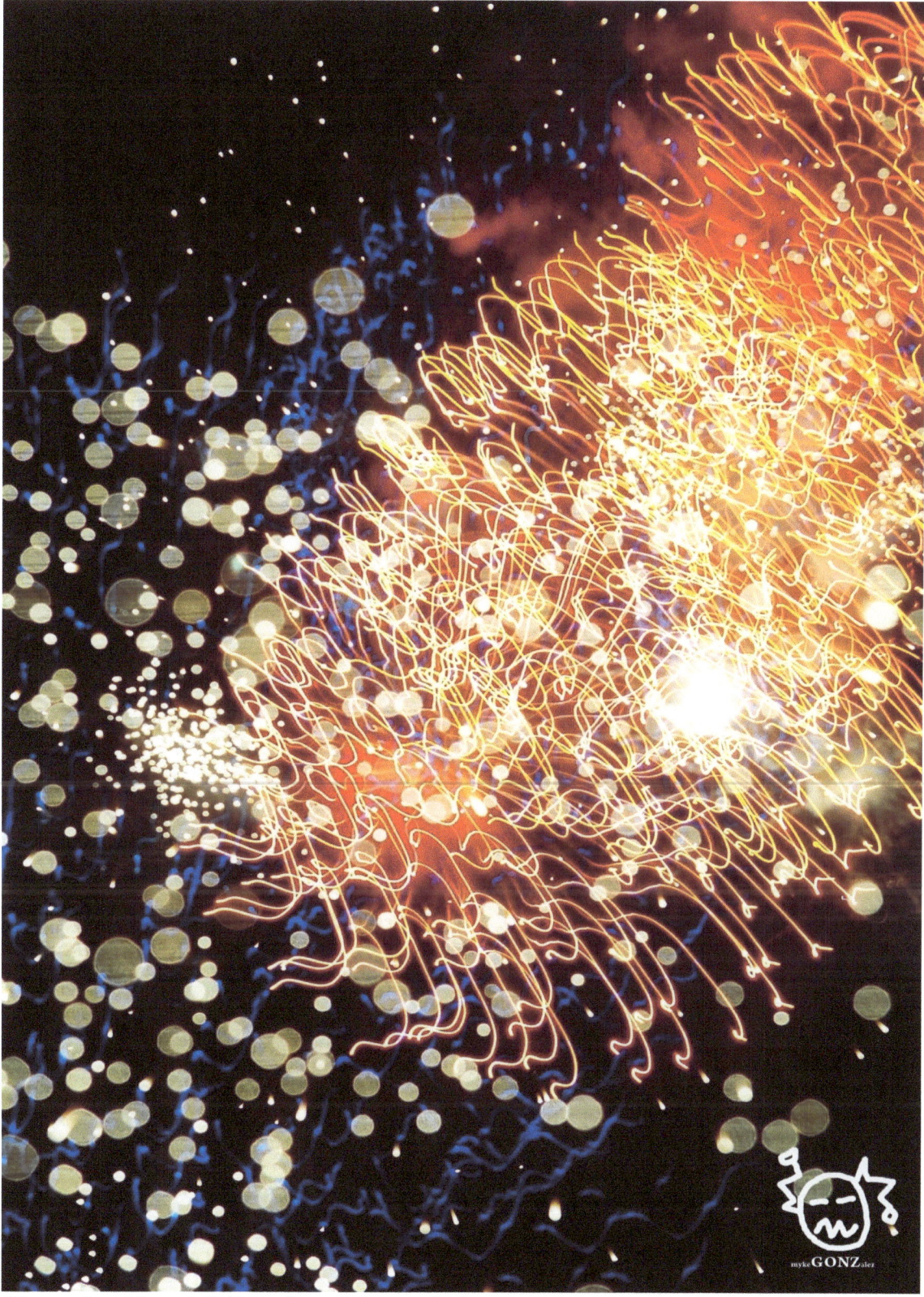

"Space Age Material" Bay city, mi fire works long exposure

Readjust and humble up.

Give a whole lot of fucks.

A whole lotta love.

Do what you can to muster up the most,

from the riches of your inherently provactative,

and beautiful soul.

Profound Whatever.

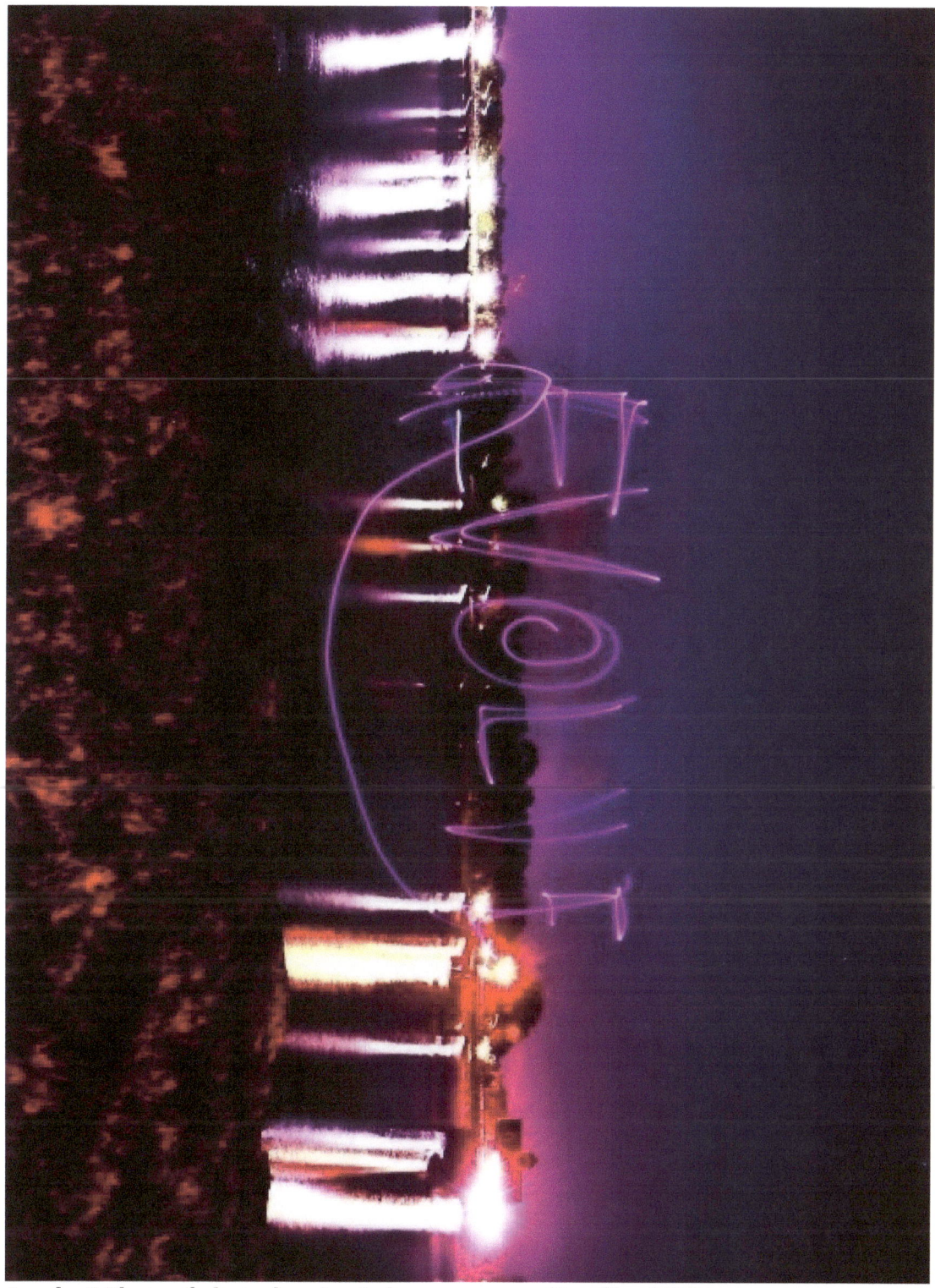

"evolve" Photo of photo drawing in long exposure. Bay City, Michigan

Freestyle to the rain drops.

A tilt of the hat to the passion that:

raised

my

b.p.m

and all that jazz,

and all the funk,

the language that we have.

The culture of our lips,

of our minds.

Freestyles to the clocks.

Profound Whatever.

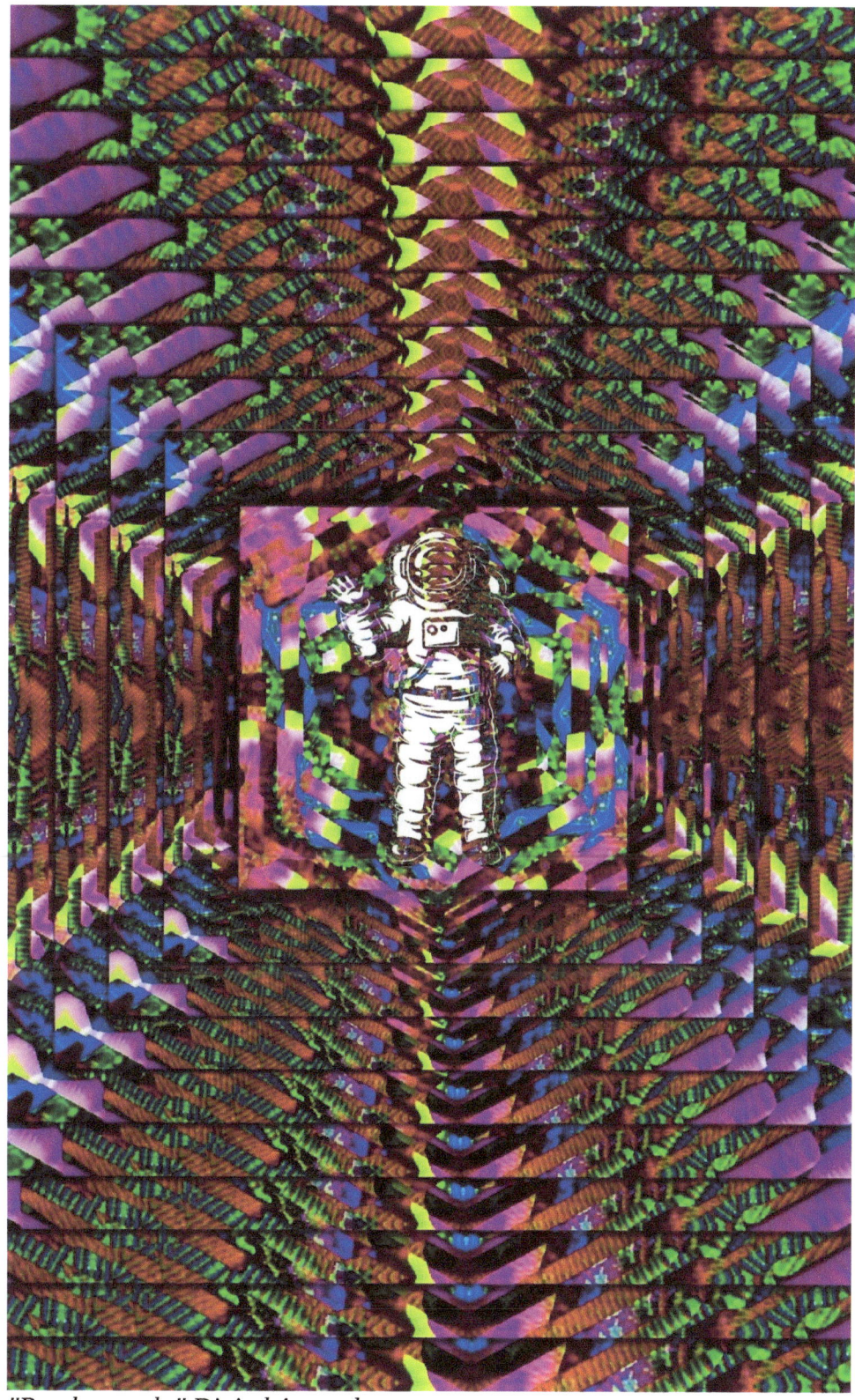

"Psychonaught" Digital Artwork

Profound Whatever.

I appreciate YOU

Profound Whatever.

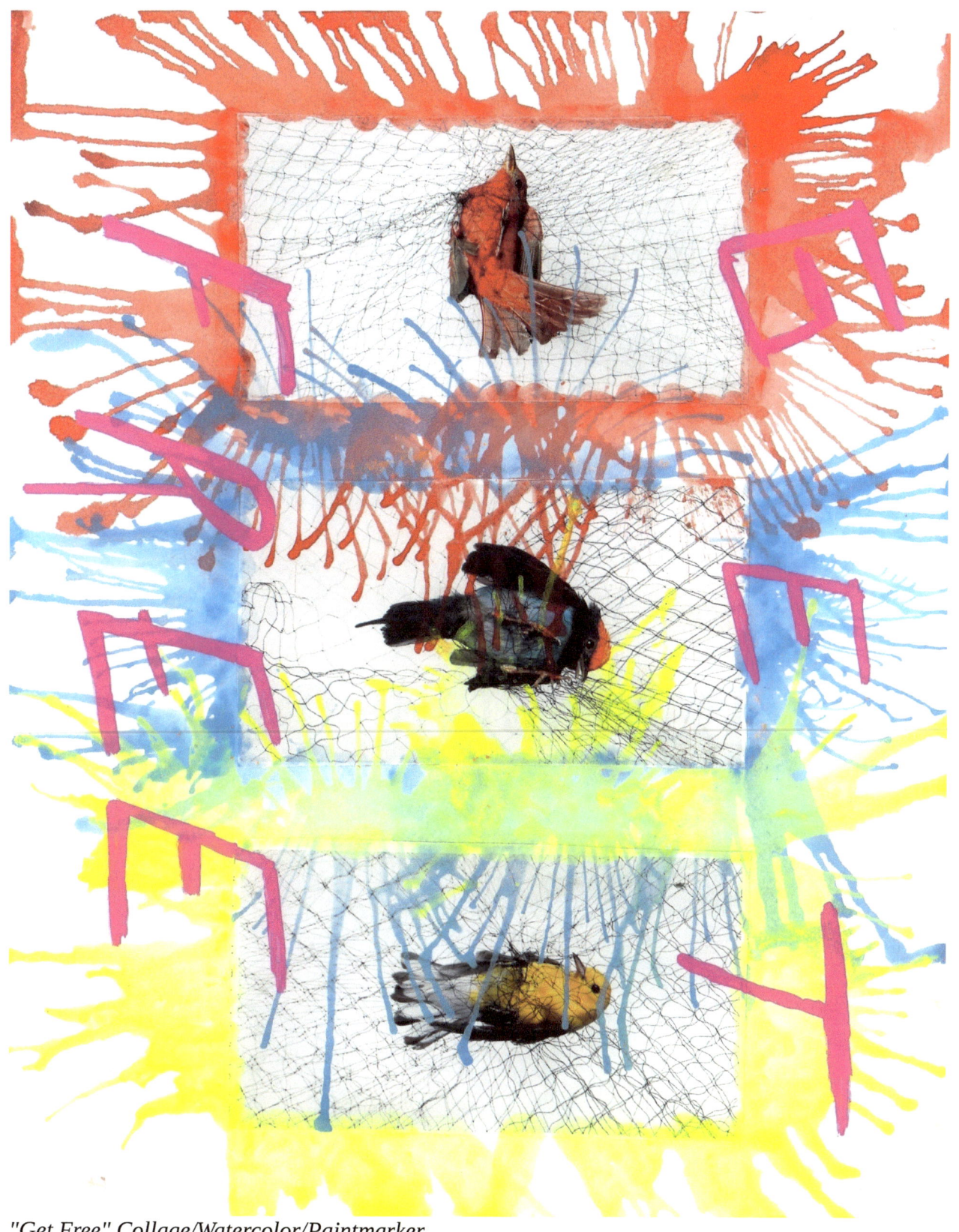

"Get Free" Collage/Watercolor/Paintmarker

STOP BITCHING
and
MANIFEST THE DREAM.

Profound Whatever.

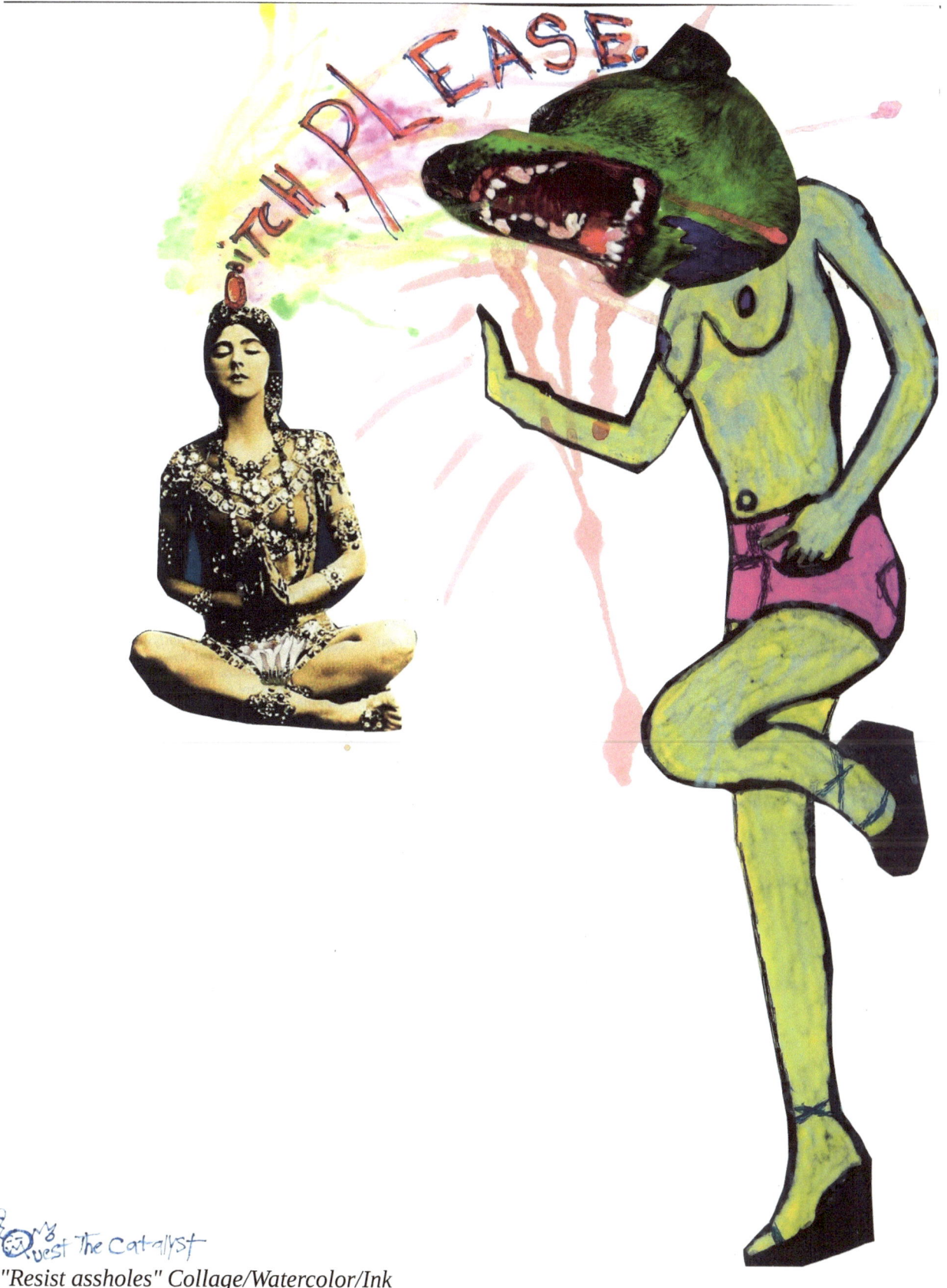

"Resist assholes" Collage/Watercolor/Ink

Profound Whatever.

Life is just and art form.

And you should really art more.

Document the moment.

Remember.

Expand,

express, cultivate, confess.

You are the ever-present, and ever-fleeting now.

You are this, and that, and all around,

You are the seed, and the dirt on the ground.

You are the ever-changing wonder of what is.

The ever-growing numbers of minutes gone by.

This gift.

This life.

MAKE IT.

MANIFEST the best intent with that beat mess,

hidden within your chest.

Be you,

That is your best.

www.ingramcontent.com/pod-product-compliance
Lightning Source LLC
Chambersburg PA
CBHW042323250526
R18347300001B/R183473PG45473CBX00026B/27